Fantastic Planet

By Katharine Kenah

School Specialty
Publishing
Columbus, Ohio

Library of Congress Cataloging-in-Publication Data is on file with the publisher.

Send all inquiries to:
School Specialty Publishing
8720 Orion Place

Where on earth are the
hottest, coldest,
highest, deepest,
largest, and smallest places?

Turn the page to find out.

The Strongest Wind

Where on earth is the strongest wind?
The strongest wind ever recorded hit
a weather station in New Hampshire.
It recorded a wind of 231 miles per hour!
This is faster than most race cars.

The Highest Waterfall

Where on earth is the highest waterfall?
The highest waterfall is in South America.
It is called *Angel Falls*.
It is over 3,000 feet tall,
the length of ten football fields!

The Largest Desert

Where on earth is the largest desert?
The largest desert is in North Africa.
It is called the *Sahara Desert*.
For thousands of miles, there is little
to see but sand.

The Largest Island

Where on earth is the largest island?
The largest island is in the
Atlantic Ocean.
It is called *Greenland*.
Greenland is covered with ice.
It is three times bigger than Texas!

The Deepest Lake

Where on earth is the deepest lake?
The deepest lake is in Russia.
It is called *Lake Baikal*.
It is deeper than the Grand Canyon!

The Largest Coral Reef

Where on earth is the largest coral reef?
The largest coral reef is in Australia.
It is called the *Great Barrier Reef*.
It is 1,240 miles long,
the distance from Chicago to Miami.

The Longest River

Where on earth is the longest river?
The longest river is in Africa.
It is called the *Nile River*.
It flows for more than 4,000 miles,
the length of South America!

The Most Active Volcano

Where on earth is the most
active volcano?
The most active volcano is in Hawaii.
It is called *Kilauea*.
It has been erupting since 1983!

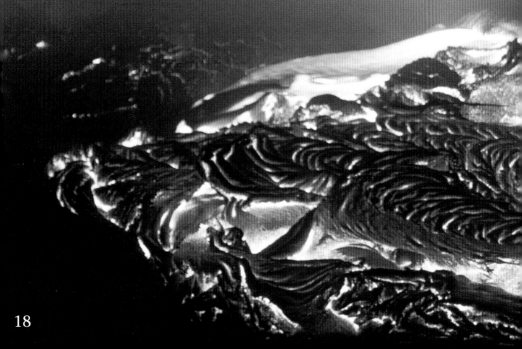

The Longest Cave

Where on earth is the longest cave?
The longest cave is in Kentucky.
It is called *Mammoth Cave*.
There are lakes, rivers, and waterfalls
inside it.

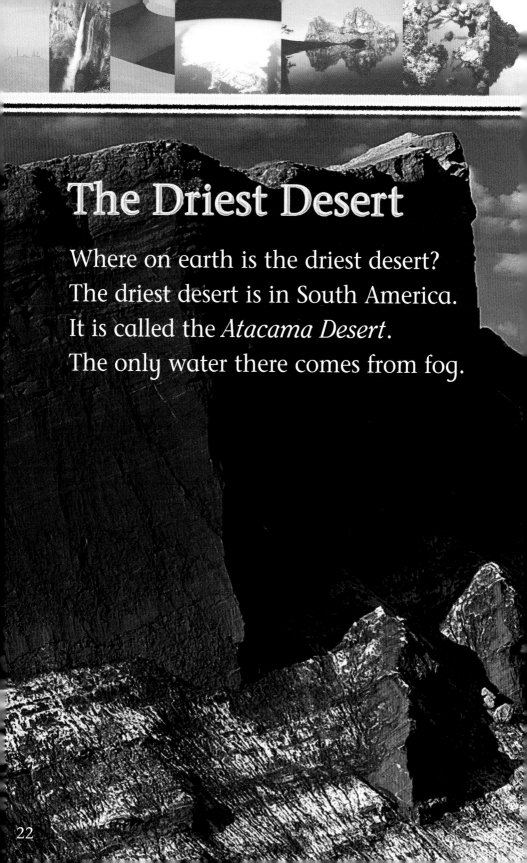

The Driest Desert

Where on earth is the driest desert?
The driest desert is in South America.
It is called the *Atacama Desert*.
The only water there comes from fog.

The Deepest Canyon

Where on earth is the deepest canyon?
The deepest canyon is in
South America.
It is called *Colca Canyon*.
It is two miles deep!

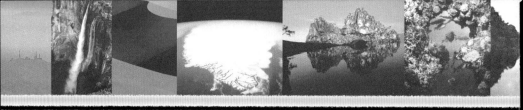

The Hottest and Coldest Places

Where on earth are the hottest
and coldest places?
The hottest place is in North America.
It is called *Death Valley*.
The coldest place is at the bottom
of the world.
It is the continent Antarctica.

The Smallest and Largest Continents

Where on earth are the smallest
and largest continents?
The largest continent is Asia.
One-third of the world's land is in Asia.
The smallest continent is Australia.
It is the only country that is also
a continent.

The Largest and Smallest Oceans

Where on earth are the largest and smallest oceans?

The largest ocean is the Pacific Ocean. It covers more than one-third of the world.

The smallest ocean is the Arctic Ocean. It is almost all ice.

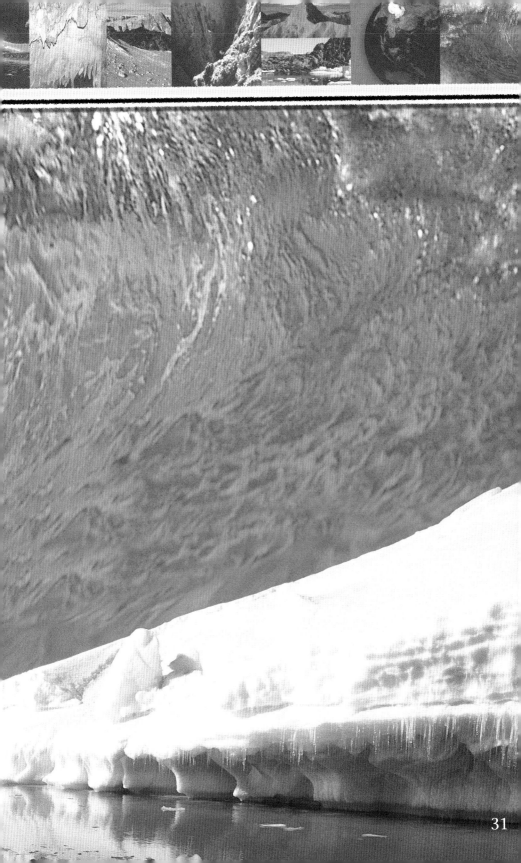

EXTREME FACTS ABOUT FANTASTIC PLANET!

- In 1934, Mount Washington Observatory measured a wind gust of 231 miles per hour, which is still the world record!

- Angel Falls was named after an American pilot, Jimmy Angel.

- The Sahara Desert covers 3.5 million square miles.

- Greenland is not all green. Thick ice covers 85 percent of the land.

- Lake Baikal contains one-fifth of the total fresh water on earth

- Certain starfish are destroying new growth on the Great Barrier Reef by eating the living coral.

- The Nile Delta in Africa is big enough to be seen from space.

- Kilauea is said to be the home of Pele, the volcano goddess of ancient Hawaiian legends.

- Mammoth Cave is 350 miles long.

- Rain has never been recorded in some parts of the Atacama Desert!

- Colca Canyon is 11,000 feet deep, twice as deep as the Grand Canyon.

- In 1913, the recorded temperature in Death Valley was 134 degrees.

- Asia covers more than 17 million square miles and has more people than any other continent.

- After crossing the stormy Atlantic, Ferdinand Magellan named the next ocean *Pacific*, meaning "peaceful".